At the Construction Site

Look, a Bulldozer!

T0019695

By Julia Jaske

A bulldozer can push.

A bulldozer can level.

 A bulldozer can push soil.

A bulldozer can level soil.

6

A bulldozer can push dirt.

A bulldozer can level dirt.

 A bulldozer can push sand.

A bulldozer can level sand.

 A bulldozer can push rocks.

A bulldozer can level rocks.

A bulldozer can push mud.

A bulldozer can level mud.

Word List

bulldozer soil rocks

push dirt mud

level sand

A bulldozer can push.

A bulldozer can level.

A bulldozer can push soil.

A bulldozer can level soil.

A bulldozer can push dirt.

A bulldozer can level dirt.

A bulldozer can push sand.

A bulldozer can level sand.

A bulldozer can push rocks.

A bulldozer can level rocks.

A bulldozer can push mud.

A bulldozer can level mud.

CHERRY BLOSSOM PRESS

Published in the United States of America by Cherry Lake Publishing Group
Ann Arbor, Michigan
www.cherrylakepublishing.com

Photo Credits: © Valentin Valkov/Shutterstock, cover, 1, 14; © photka/Shutterstock, back cover; © LETOPISEC/Shutterstock, 2; © Juan Enrique del Barrio/Shutterstock, 3; © LETOPISEC/Shutterstock, 4; © LETOPISEC/Shutterstock, 5; © Maksim Safaniuk/Shutterstock, 6; © ghornephoto/istock, 7; © serato/Shutterstock, 8; © ewg3D/istock, 9; © SERGEI PRIMAKOV/Shutterstock, 10; © Maksim Safaniuk/Shutterstock, 11; © CjVitoS/Shutterstock, 12; © CjVitoS/Shutterstock, 13

Cherry Blossom Press is an imprint of Cherry Lake Publishing Group.

Library of Congress Cataloging-in-Publication Data

Names: Jaske, Julia, author.
Title: Look, a bulldozer! / by Julia Jaske.
Description: Ann Arbor, Michigan : Cherry Lake Publishing, [2021] | Series:
    At the construction site
Identifiers: LCCN 2021007865 (print) | LCCN 2021007866 (ebook) | ISBN
    9781534188198 (paperback) | ISBN 9781534189591 (pdf) | ISBN
    9781534190993 (ebook)
Subjects: LCSH: Earthwork–Juvenile literature. | Bulldozers–Juvenile
    literature.
Classification: LCC TA735 .J373 2021 (print) | LCC TA735 (ebook) | DDC
    621.8/65–dc23
LC record available at https://lccn.loc.gov/2021007865
LC ebook record available at https://lccn.loc.gov/2021007866

Printed in the United States of America
Corporate Graphics